THE CHIP

and How it Changed the World

Ian Locke

SIMON & SCHUSTER
YOUNG BOOKS

First published in 1994 by
Simon & Schuster Young Books

Text copyright © 1994 Ian Locke
Illustrations copyright © 1994 Simon & Schuster Young Books
Simon & Schuster Young Books
Campus 400
Maylands Avenue
Hemel Hempstead
Herts
HP2 7EZ

A CIP catalogue record for this book is available from the British Library

ISBN 07500 1514 4

Commissioning Editor: Thomas Keegan
Editor: Christopher Norris
Designer: Vivienne Gordon
Illustrators: Peter Bull
             Ann John
             Colin Meir
             Julia Osorno

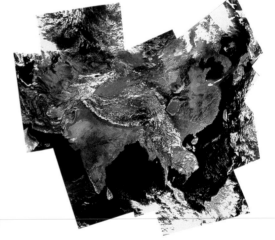

Picture Acknowledgements:
The publishers would like to thank the following for their permission to use
copyright material:
The Advertising Archives: p19b; The Bridgeman Art Library: pp8-9, 12, 15t, 161, 33b;
Colorific!: pp25, 43t; E.T. Archive: p11t; Robert Harding Picture Library: pp9bl, 19t,
281, 29t; The Hulton Deutsch Collection: pp141, 15bl + r, 18, 21c, 34; Robert Hunt
Photo Library; p171; IBM; p35br; The Imperial War Museum: p16b; Sylvia Katz: p38;
The Kobal Collection: pp26, 43c; Ian Locke: pp8r, 9br, 10b, 13 (both), 14r, 19c, 20b,
24, 40; The Linnear Library, London/Eileen Tweedy; pp32, 37; Nissan Cars, Tokyo; p22;
Popperfoto; pp17r, 21t, 28r; Redferns: p41b; Rex Features; 35bl, 41t, 43b; The Science
Museum, London: pp11b, 33t; The Science Photo Library; pp81, 20t, 21, 23 (both), 35t,
36, 37tl + b, 38-39, 40-41; Syndication International: p27b; Wellcome Institute,
Oxford: p42.

Typeset by: Bob Gordon Design and Goodfellow and Egan Ltd, Cambridge
Printed and bound in Hong Kong

CONTENTS

Beginnings   8

Broadening Vision   10

Keeping Tabs   12

I Spy   14

Breaking the Code   16

Big Blue   18

We Never Close   20

Massive Reductions   22

Home from Home   24

It's All a Game   26

Market Control   28

Robotics   30

Seeing Signs   32

Getting Close   34

Healthy Living   36

Selling to Millions   38

All Together   40

Future Worlds   42

Glossary   44

Index   45

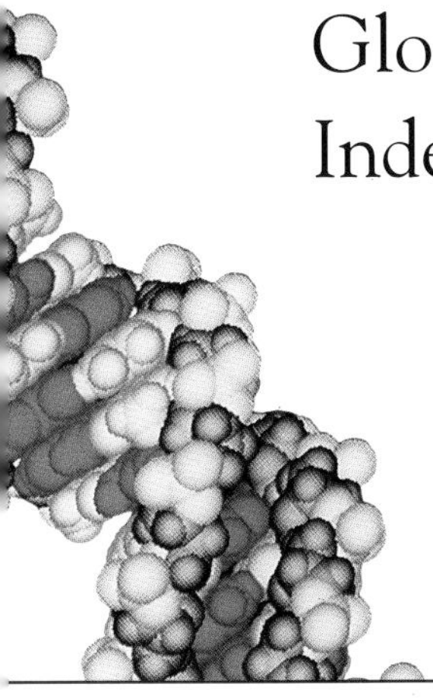

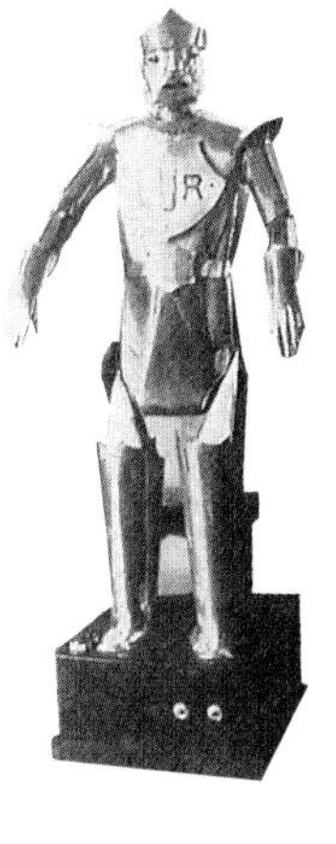

All living things have a life span. This might be seconds or a very long time. Early humankind had certain weaknesses because of the way in which the species evolved. They could not see well at night so life could only be sustained by activity during daylight. The extent of other physical limits were probably tried out by early humans, bringing success or failure. Some idea of space (three dimensions), distance (two dimensions) and quantity (number), either on their own or in combination helped the survival of the species.

In the 16th and 17th centuries telescopes, such as this German Bessel telescope, began to be used to explore space, challenging Ancient Greek ideas about the universe.

Gods in the heavens

Humans have big memories and an awareness that events take place, including the appearance and disappearance of light. By 2000 BC the relationship between night and day and the sun was beginning to be understood. The sun was seen to be vital to life and became an object of worship. Other objects in the sky, day and night, were identified and also made Gods. Events in the heavens followed a pattern that coincided with what took place on earth. This was a crucial observation. Among the peoples who saw this were the Egyptians, the Maya of South America and the Babylonians in the Middle East. Records of this cycle were made involving signs and symbols. They were used to regulate daily life. The Ancient Egyptians became the first to divide the day into 24 hours. Some signs and symbols were numbers, to represent objects or events in the real world. The Maya evolved a system where numbers related each other to form a calendar. Over the centuries three different areas of the world were at the focus of mathematics – Greece, India and Arabia.

Ptolomy's Universe, 1559. In the 16th century, the ancient Greek view of the universe was replaced by new ideas.

The arrival of tables

The Romans invented their own numerical system using base 10 and adopted a number of familiar signs, such as £ (Libra). For counting units the Greeks and Romans used pebbles or discs of glass, ivory or bone, known as calculi. For day to day calculation they adopted a table, called the abacus on which the units were placed. This was the origin of the idea of tables for calculation.

Mathematics

The Greeks developed a system of symbols for natural structures, called geometry, which defined the relationships between two-dimensional images, three-dimensional structures and space, such as buildings, and distance. Pythagorus proved that the real world could be governed by exact numbers. This led to models of the heavens, called astrolobes which laid out the stars in a sphere. In the Middle East the Babylonians invented digits and the notion of computation. Computation was the process of adding, subtracting and dividing numbers. This process was step by step and was distinct from the Greek approach. Any number could be used as a base for computation, to represent a scale of quantity. The choice of this base had a great impact on civilizations. The more uncommon the base, the more difficult it was to pass on the knowledge. The adoption of the base 10 in the ancient world gave a clear advantage over the Maya, who used 5, 20 and 360. In India, the Hindus began trading links with the Arabs, overcoming dangerous journeys over land or sea. They saw the collection of astronomical tables to guide their route as important.

Above: The earliest examples of mathematics arose in the Middle East. The knowledge was shared through signs, such as on this Babylonian tablet of 500 BC.

Mathematics was used to shape the magnificent monuments of ancient Greece and Egypt, such as the Parthenon and Sphinx.

As trade and currency spread around the ancient world, mathematics remained limited to the step-by-step approach. The Arabs devised numerals to make the process easier. The measurement of time and space added to understanding, but demanded a system to cope with parts of numbers. The answer was proposed by the Arab Alkarisimi in about AD 830 who wrote a book on algebra (a form of arithmetic in which letters express quantities and signs represent operations). It also introduced the first decimals.

Trading in numbers

Astronomy and maths were particularly important to the Arabs. Much of the Arab world had no natural landmarks and had a harsh climate. However, at night the sky was often clear. Mechanical calendars were constructed to assist travellers, and these got to Europe in about AD 800. Because of the influence of the church, Roman development of language and number was severely limited. This changed in 1202 when the Italian mathematician Leonardo Fibonacci explained the arabic numerals and Italy became the first country in the West to use the system. In the 1500s the Chinese introduced the abacus, the first digital computer, to Russia and Japan. In Europe all non-mental arithmetic was done by placing counters on boards. The idea of zero only came in AD 876. As the population increased, demand for larger quantities of material or products and also payment for these increased. Arabic numerals were more suitable for calculating large numbers than Roman numerals. They spread throughout Europe. Gerber, later Pope Sylvester II, proposed another approach – the arrangement of figures in columns so that sub-totals could be calculated.

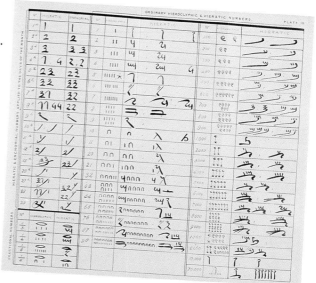

Ancient Egyptians evolved a complex sign language for numbers which helped set up and maintain their civilization. Some of these numbers, as this table shows, hardly changed for thousands of years.

Money lenders and borrowers in 14th century Europe. As government of people became more widespread in Europe the first counting houses for tax and banking were formed. The earliest examples were in Italy.

Calculating the future

Investigation of a new source of power called electricity was carried out in the 1830s. This was based on common materials like copper and magnets. The link between engineering and electricity became a possibility. The vastly improved quality of precision instruments, such as lathes, required the application of mathematics. In 1875 a new way of presenting time was shown by Sir William Thomson's machine to predict tides and heights of high water, operated by cranks and pulleys. In 1888 the American, Oberlin Smith, proposed an extraordinary idea for such tasks – magnetic data storage.

The age of exploration

Western trade and exploration involved travelling ever increasing distances. The demand for accurate reference tables for surveying and navigation of journeys led to the invention of logarithms by John Napier in about 1600 and the first analogue calculator, the slide rule. In 1671 the Dutchman, Gottfried Liebnitz, suggested using machines for calculation to save time. He had one built for multiplication in 1694, basing it on an earlier mechanical device devised by the Frenchman, Blaise Pascal, which operated by a series of gears. The machine was ahead of its time. In 1822 a brilliant Englishman called Charles Babbage devised a calculating machine to help the government deal with two problems – tax and economic statistics. In 1833 the project was nearing its conclusion and Babbage adopted the idea of punch cards to 'programme' the machine. These had been invented in France by Jaquard to operate his power loom. The government of the day then withdrew backing for Babbage and his machine was virtually forgotten. Only two of his ideas survived – the speedometer and actuarial tables, for working out life insurance premiums and returns.

Englishman Charles Babbage's difference engine, the world's first large workable computer, was reconstructed in London 150 years after his death, proving Babbage's extraordinary vision.

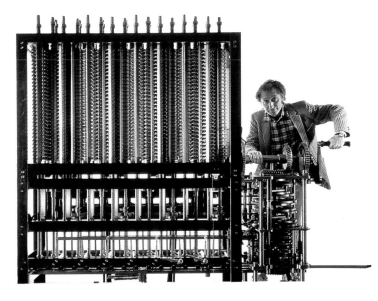

After William the Conqueror became King of England in 1066, he wanted a record of the places and people that he ruled. The result was the Domesday Book, which was out of date by the time it was finished. It forecast how much money might be raised in taxes and the people who might pose a threat to the king. Such rough estimates were used by governments up until the 18th century. When single rulers began to be replaced by Parliaments, decisions increasingly depended on plans. Some knowledge of arithmetic was necessary to understand them and so books of instruction appeared.

The Domesday Book, begun after the arrival of Wiliam the Conqueror in Britain in 1066, was the first full record or database of England.

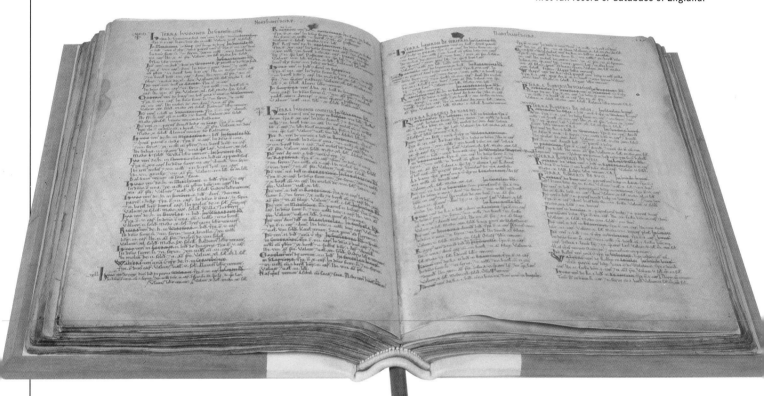

Mapping the future

By 1700 surveys and plans of the known world had re-appeared, to satisfy the demand for details of peoples and their likely wealth. Exploitation of crops and minerals was made possible by accurate measurements, using rulers, compasses and other instruments. This allowed engineers to build machines for certain jobs and scientists to understand the natural world better. The growth in trade in the 1800s made instruction books for building machines common.

Specialists emerged, among them accountants and technicians. Governments needed to know more about such change in nations. The approach, the census, was invented by the Swedes. It was a measurement of population, work and production of a country, to be used for planning public services. This approach proved popular, and soon smaller surveys of people and what they did took place, leading to the modern business of polling.

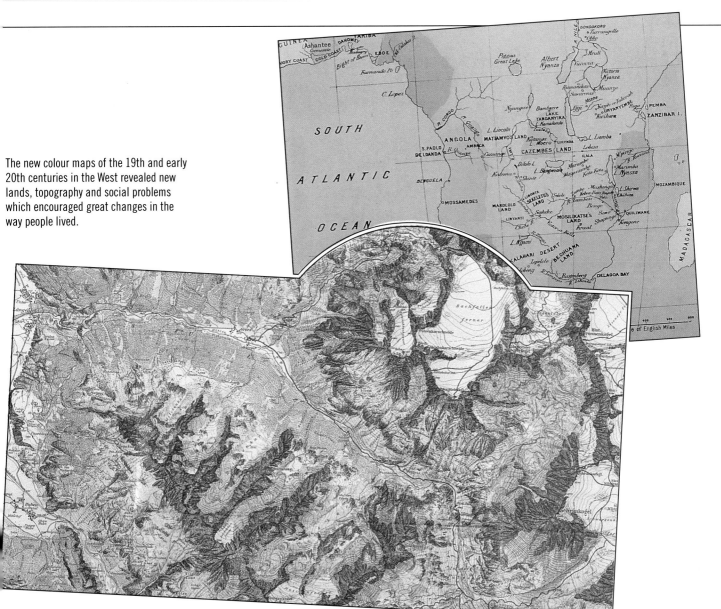

The new colour maps of the 19th and early 20th centuries in the West revealed new lands, topography and social problems which encouraged great changes in the way people lived.

Social science

The data from land surveying became maps. Distance and relative location were defined by the scales and grids. From 1870 common signs were used to identify landmarks on the maps, such as a blue line for a river. The world of politics depended on such detailed data and drawings. They identified the sources of cholera in London in the 1870s, leading to a cure. Charles Booth, conducting his own surveys, produced maps of wealth and poverty in London which led to the clearance of slums in 1901. This type of work became known as social science. The same concept of data and image gave rise to modern advertising and marketing businesses.

Number crunching

Mechanical assistance for processing data was soon needed. It came with the tabulator invented by an American, Herman Hollerith. He discovered the key to its success while on a tram. A conductor punched his ticket with holes representing his height, weight and colouring. Hollerith began work on his machine to tabulate data using a set of hole-punched cards in 1880. It was ready in 1889 and used in the US Census of 1890. Other governments soon used the machines. Companies that produced cash register machines, such as NCR and TMC, added computing machines to their products. They developed the use of modern sales techniques.

Once printing became common in the West from the 16th century onwards, translation proved to be one of the simplest and most effective methods of transferring the knowledge of one culture to another over distance. However, there were some things that were not meant to be shared. By 1850 nations at war in Europe had realized the value of such information for the keeping of stability at home and for ruling empires.

Leonardo's notebooks of the 14th century were written backwards to disguise their contents. They were readable when reflected in a mirror.

Right: Numbers were widely used in the 15th century. Here they helped to teach music.

Intelligence tests

Trying to keep information from enemies has existed for centuries. Leonardo da Vinci disguised his writings and inventions by using mirror writing, while the English diarist Samuel Pepys invented shorthand that was only deciphered in the 1860s. In the 16th century simple numerical codes matching the letters of the alphabet to numbers had been used. In the 19th century Western governments established separate intelligence forces to counter threats to the interests of the nation. These forces were the secret services. They were better organized than the single spies employed by governments in the past.

French soldiers of the 19th century. Until 1870 the army used few spies.

The arrival of Morse

The spies of the 18th century used their wits to survive. They included the architect of Blenheim Palace, Sir John Vanburgh, and adventurers like John Paul Jones in America and Fenimore Cooper in Canada. The setting up of trained police forces worldwide made this amateur approach outdated. In 1870 a German called William Stieber devised a new system at the outbreak of the Franco–Prussian War. Key French military secrets were discovered by Frenchmen paid by the Prussian Government to send information back to Berlin. A centralized network was established providing ready information under a single command. The German success prompted France to set up the Deuxieme Bureau – and Britain followed suit with the Military Intelligence Section (MI5) in 1909 and the Committee of Imperial Defence. Russia established an external and internal organization for intelligence (a tradition continued by the KGB and NKVD after the communist revolution of 1917). The success of these organizations depended on a flow of reliable information. At the outbreak of World War I in 1914, Britain and France had rapidly increased their range of intelligence services as they faced threats from anarchists and terrorists, and an army of German spies. Direct exchange of information by post or courier was overtaken by new technologies. The first was Morse Code, invented by the former American painter Samuel Morse in 1835. Telegraphs transmitted sound by breaking or joining an electric current. The resulting sounds were translated from dots and dashes into letters.

A new revolution

The US government quickly recognized the importance of telegraphy and backed the system. Its success worldwide influenced all industries, laying the foundations for rapid global communication once international agreement was reached on Morse Code and its use. Another major development was the telephone, invented by Alexander Graham Bell. The system involved the use of a telephone numbers and relied on a connection system. As the telephone grew in popularity, the jumble of different codes and companies were sorted out by international agreement, and most telephone systems came under government control. Just as the telegraph and telephone gained wide acceptance by 1900, a new revolution in distance communication called radio was started by a young Italian, Guglielmo Marconi.

A group of American soldiers received wireless messages during World War I. Wireless was widely used during the war for intelligence operations.

Troops marching up to the fighting line somewhere in France'. Detailed intelligence of operations during World War I was limited by armies for security reasons.

BREAKING THE CODE

In 1900 Britain controlled the world's largest shipping fleet and empire, both relying on international communication for their maintenance. After tests of Marconi's invention from ship to shore, the British Admiralty backed its introduction. Like the telephone, the radio relied on a numerical system for operation. Broadcasts could be received by tuning the radio receiver to a particular frequency. Up to the 1920s one broad waveband, as it was called, was used – long wave. It was followed by short wave and FM. On the outbreak of World War I use of telecommunications in intelligence was limited. Reliance on postal services in Britain and Germany led to inefficient spying as secrets proved difficult to keep.

Gulgielmo Marconi (1874–1937), the Italian inventor revolutionized world communication with the introduction of the wireless from 1900.

Figuring it out

An exception was Admiral 'Blinker' Hall of British naval intelligence. He arranged for direct German telegraph cables to America to be cut in 1914, forcing the Germans either to use a link which ran through Britain or to use wireless. All transmissions were monitored. After a German code book was captured, a mathematician, Sir Alfred Ewing, was hired to decipher the code. In 1917 Britain intercepted and decoded the Zimmerman telegram. This declared Germany's intention to begin sinking all vessels and, if the USA entered the war as a result, to join forces with Mexico and Japan to reconquer Texas, New Mexico and Arizona. The message had been sent by Western Union, the US telegraph company, direct to Mexico. Britain persuaded the company to forward a copy to the US ambassador in London giving him access to the German codes to prove the truth of the message. The German threat persuaded the USA to enter the war, making an Allied victory possible.

The sinking of the liner, the *Lusitania* on 7 May 1915 is often given as the cause of America's entry to World War I. However, an equal contribution to this decision was information provided by code breakers and the Allied intelligence services.

Enigma

In Lucerne, Switzerland, the British spy Alexander Foote and a Swiss publisher, Rudolf Roesser, broadcast data direct to Moscow. Their source was a key figure in the German High Command. The information was received directly from German sources, then encoded and decoded twice, requiring extreme care.

In 1938, Germany began making random code machines in Poland. Polish agents sent parts of these Enigma codes to England and France. At war, both Britain and France obtained whole machines. In England a brilliant mathematician called Alan Turing headed a team to decipher these German codes.

The rise of espionage

With the value of intelligence now proved, specialist code-breaking units were set up between the wars and scientists employed on the work. Marconi, for example, worked on short-wave radio, which was harder to intercept. The use of seemingly random numbers as the basis of codes required great dedication and insight. They became a central means of communicating with spies. During the 1930s one of the most brilliant agents was the Russian, Richard Sorge. As a trusted journalist, he used short-wave radio or microfilm to send a stream of data from Japan. In 1941, he warned Russia of the imminent German invasion of the USSR and a year later was able to prove that Japan was intent on an attack on the USA rather than Russia. This intelligence saved the Soviet Union from defeat. Since short-wave transmission became detectable, Sorge took to broadcasting from a motor cruiser off the coast, holding parties on board to cover his movements. He and his spy ring were caught by the Japanese in 1942 and he was executed in 1944.

The unprovoked attack on Pearl Harbor by the Japanese on 7 December 1941, in which over 2000 Americans were killed, was a disaster for the American intelligence services. It brought America into the World War II.

German forces using the Enigma coding machine (seen in the foreground). Used for many communications, the cracking of German codes gave the Allies a crucial advantage during the World War II.

Up to the 1840s the only national means of regular communication was by printed newspapers or courier. In business, this meant relying on horses, runners or ships. Railways and steam-power for ships improved the flow of information. Electric telegraphs made business news widely available in the 1860s, improving commerce throughout the world. The appearance of dictionaries, encyclopaedias, international language and universal male education all helped. The illegibility of much business paperwork remained a problem. The answer lay in a hand-operated standard printing machine – the typewriter.

The earliest working typewriters were made by the rifle manufacturer Remington in the USA. The standard Remington machine of 1878 introduced the lower case (small, rather than capital letters).

A problem with writing

The typewriter was not a new idea. The first patent had been granted in England in 1714. The necessity for such a machine was influenced by several factors in the USA. The extension of railways across the continent required the formation of large groups of investors or shareholders. The resources needed for the railways were huge and suppliers sent material from home and abroad. Across the world the railway boom combined speculation and fraud. Fortunes could be made or lost in 'railway mania'. The number of suppliers of faulty goods rose, accidents increased. Governments acted quickly, introducing a range of laws to control business operations. Such legislation, starting in the USA, demanded proper and regular records of business activity. Up to the 1840s business records were entirely written by hand, using pen and ink. In an attempt to improve legibility, copy books were introduced in schools, leading to 'Copperplate writing' after the original copper plates used in printing such books. This worked in places like Britain or France and their empires. The USA faced a different problem.

The typewriter

English was not the first language for much of the US population. A way had to be found of presenting clear written messages in English. In Milwaukee, Charles Scholes produced the first modern typewriter in 1868. It was manufactured by Remingtons, the rifle-makers. At first it produced only capital letters, until a shift key made lower case possible in 1878. The roll bar producing type which could be read as it was done, appeared in 1883. The Querty arrangement of keys was adopted to stop the key bars from sticking at speed. The typewriter encouraged stationers to issue standard-sized paper and carbon paper for legible copies to be stored.

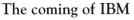

New types of work

By 1890 the typewriter was widely used for letters and documents, but could not deal with columns. It provided employment and affected the whole approach to work. The term office was applied to tailor-made buildings, causing a vast change to the appearance of cities like San Francisco or Tokyo. Business districts became defined, such as Wall Street in New York City or The City of London. The location of a business headquarters was often distant from factories. This divide, which the typewriter helped create, led to new terms for types of work – white collar and blue collar.

Modern Tokyo and Tokyo as it was in about 1880. In just over a century the revolution in electronics brought about a huge change in the face of the world's major cities and the conduct of business.

The coming of IBM

Electric power greatly improved office machinery. In 1914 Thomas Watson of CTR in the USA established an experimental department to work on new machines. In 1924 it became known as IBM. The company introduced the first automatic printer and ideas such as making a market for a product. In 1933 IBM helped two scientists Dr Eckert and Howard Aiken with mathematical problems, by building a new calculator at Harvard University – the Mark 1 with 800,000 parts. It was the basis of the computer. Through the war IBM produced much of the machinery which controlled the US Army and its machine was able to crack the Japanese naval codes in 1944.

The first computers were large and used many thousands of parts. The world's leading manufacturer and pioneer of the modern main frame computer was the American company IBM, known as Big Blue.

After World War II had ended, the peace of the world only seemed possible by the great powers forming an international body to exchange information – the new United Nations Organization – and by having a common defence policy. Language differences were a big problem, but the war had demonstrated that co-operation was possible. New technologies based on mathematical theories had been crucial to the fate of the world. Through the UN, agreements were made to bring standards to international communication and business. Many decisions and developments relied on numerical data.

Electronic storage

Science and business encouraged further work on the computer. In June 1946, US mathematicians John von Neumann and Oskar Morgenstein published the idea of a 'stored programme' for an 'Electronic Computing Instrument'. The earlier ENIAC and Colossus computers relied on external memory, with an operator plugging in cables. By 1950 they had completed the EDVAC or 'Electronic Variable Automatic Computer'. Under a team headed by Turing, Manchester University completed another electronic computer, EDSAC. The Russians completed their first computer within a year. Many companies began developing computers with stored memories. The possibility that each company would invent their own computer language was real. In the West the US Defense Department backed the development of COBOL (Common Business Oriented Language) to counter the problem. In 1954 an IBM team began work on another standard language, Fortran (Formula Translation), which opened the way to understanding between machines.

The transistor

The first commercial computer, the Ferranti Star, was produced in Britain in 1950. The machine cost a fortune, had thousands of parts and had limited capacity. The magnetic core could store only 60–10,000 words, demanding expert input of data. In the US Eckert and Mauchly successfully launched the Univac 1 (Universal Automatic Computer), produced for the 1951 census in America.

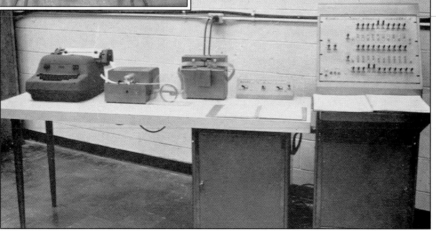

The early computers had a magnetic core, which included hundreds of magnets. The system was operated by the binary code.

By the 1960s the standard computer had become smaller, as with the IBM M3 computer, but still required a large space for its operation.

The authorities recognized that such machines had a value. By the end of the 1950s the US Defense Department found computers indispensable in the development of rocket systems, while many countries used the new machines for their census. However, computers and a whole range of electrical goods relied on large valves – airless glass tubes which, when heated, emitted tiny particles called electrons that provided a electrical current. The widening of the market became possible when transistors replaced valves. The transistor, invented in 1948, was a semiconductor in a tiny crystal case.

The arrival of a 24-hour business

The increasing use of the computer coincided with growth for telephone and telex businesses. International agreements now made it possible to link most countries with one another. This made a 24-hour service possible. Many businesses including power suppliers, airlines, post offices, banks and manufacturers moved to full-time operations. During the 1960s such links led to the rise of multinational companies which spanned the world, always open somewhere no matter what the time. Overnight communication became common, creating new patterns for jobs, opening hours of shops and transport timetables.

In the 1950s work in America and Britain linked computers with defence and space projects. The Ferranti computer was used in Britain.

Oil refining is one of the key modern industries improved by computers and electronics.

From the 1950s it was clear that electronics would be a major industry. Consumer goods began to be produced in large numbers in many parts of the world. This revolution depended on an increasing exchange of knowledge, with licence granted for the use of technologies by the patent holders. Early licensees of the new technologies were the Japanese. In 1950 the Westernization of Japan was little over a century old. By 1910 Japan had become a world power, largely through heavy industry controlled by the military. The atomic bombs of 1945 impressed on the Japanese more than other nations the power of technology.

New-look electronics

Immediately after World War II, with its heavy industries destroyed or dismantled, small businesses supported a weak Japanese economy. Companies like Sony began by licensing Western technology. Japanese culture accepted miniaturization and simple geometry. Engineers realized that transistors saved scarce raw materials and were versatile. This made cheaper products a reality. Miniaturization in the West began through espionage needs. First used in printing, microphotographs followed, being taken out of Paris during the seige of 1870 by pigeons. The two world wars speeded up the process with miniature guns, cameras and microfilm.

The Nissan assembly line. After World War II Japan developed a wide range of manufacturing industries, covering large and small products from the motor car to the cassette. It was a leading industrial nation by the 1970s.

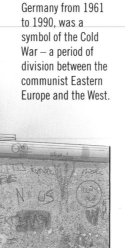

Below: The Berlin Wall. The Wall, dividing Berlin in Germany from 1961 to 1990, was a symbol of the Cold War – a period of division between the communist Eastern Europe and the West.

Looking at the minute

The Cold War resulted in experiments with miniature microphones, radios and the microdot. These developments coincided with the development of the electron microscope. This took resolution of an image from the visible to the virtually invisible. Beyond human sight, the images were transmitted to the viewer by a cathode ray tube (the basic element of a TV set), invented by the Englishman, Sir William Crookes. The manipulation of tiny particles and extreme miniaturization became possible. Some US companies began work on reductions to the size of transistorized circuits. The breakthrough came at Texas Instruments in 1959 – the microchip.

The chip

The chip is made of silicon, a semiconductor, normally a poor conductor of electricity. However, if it is mixed with tiny amounts of other materials, such as arsenic, it becomes a good conductor. This process is known as 'doping'. The chips themselves are a combination of electrical components such as transistors, capacitors and resistors, built into the surface. At the atomic level the current flows across switches which comprise the central processing unit that deals with the bits of information.

Each signal across the gate or not (carried millions of times a second) is in binary code, equivalent to an on/off switch and known as a bit. A group of eight bits together is known as a byte.

After tests, the good chips are mounted on plastic with two rows of metal pins. In 1971 a further advance was the production of a microprocessor which included the entire circuitry on a single chip.

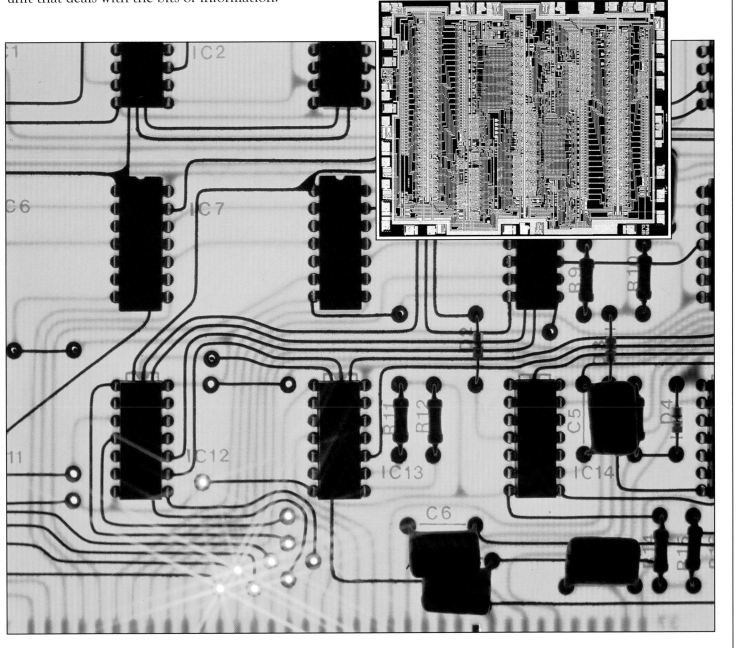

British advances in computers and early lead disappeared because possible uses appeared to be limited to research and data processing. As costs reduced and applications increased, the place of the computer within offices and industry was clear by the 1960s. It became more and more part of the office, alongside the electric typewriter, telex and calculator. The change in attitude was sparked by a design problem.

Computer graphics

Without the US defence and space programmes the continued use of computers might have remained limited. Then the Boeing aircraft company decided to model the design for the new Seattle – Tacoma airport on computer. The computer was linked to a display screen to create what Boeing called 'computer graphics'. There had been simpler graphic uses before, such as in radar tracking using the IBM Whirlwind computer, but the Boeing experiment brought the computer much closer to everyday life. Computers appeared in libraries and were used for predicting elections, for booking plane tickets and hotel reservations. These new applications brought together the telephone, telex, visual displays and typewriter to trained personnel as a single type of job. Systems were designed for specific customers. In 1965 new VDT (Video Display Terminals) were introduced. Interest in computers was reflected in a wide range of electronics magazines. The invention of the microprocessor made a cheap computer theoretically possible and in 1975 a US electronics magazine published instructions for home-made computers. The demand was huge.

The first applications of computer graphics were in the airline industry, helping not only the design of airports, but also navigation systems and the building of aircraft.

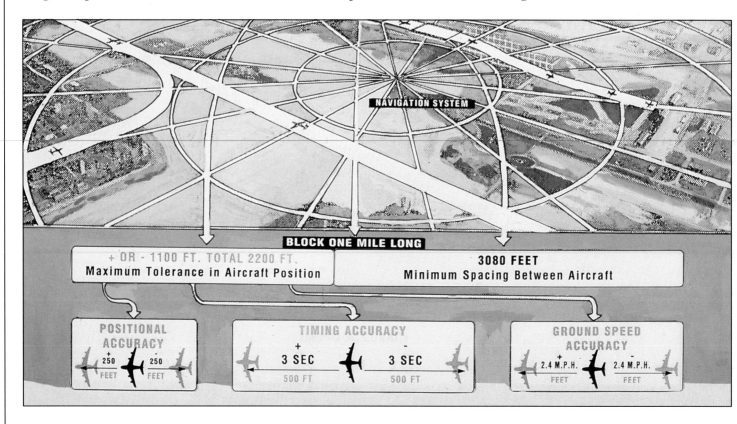

NAVIGATION SYSTEM

BLOCK ONE MILE LONG

+ OR - 1100 FT. TOTAL 2200 FT.
Maximum Tolerance in Aircraft Position

3080 FEET
Minimum Spacing Between Aircraft

POSITIONAL ACCURACY
+ 250 FEET   - 250 FEET

TIMING ACCURACY
+ 3 SEC   500 FT   - 3 SEC   500 FT

GROUND SPEED ACCURACY
+ 2.4 M.P.H. FEET   - 2.4 M.P.H. FEET

Getting personal

In 1976 two Harvard drop-outs, Steve Jobs from Atari and Steve Wozniak launched the first personal computer, the Apple, offering portable software for programming in the form of a tape or floppy disc. The portable computer opened the market to home users. It also had many professional applications. Geologists and naturalists, among others, used them on location. This encouraged a new software industry, with many amateurs challenging the established companies. The PC also made links between the telephone and other computer users through modems.

Standard language

One of the biggest initial barriers to use was the complexity of computer language. It required some knowledge of the operating systems. Two Americans, Bill Gates and Paul Allen, solved the problem with the invention of a conversational way of programming – BASIC (Beginners' All-purpose Symbolic Instruction Code) a condensed version of the language used on large computers, in 1975. It became the standard PC operating system in the 1980s, to be followed by another Microsoft programme for easy use – Windows. Given a common, universal programming language, conversations between computers became possible. The introduction of a standard put the power of the computer in the hands of individual people. This had a dramatic affect on small businesses, allowing fewer workers to control an office. They were then used by all types of services, including those of the social and emergency services, changing the organization of daily life.

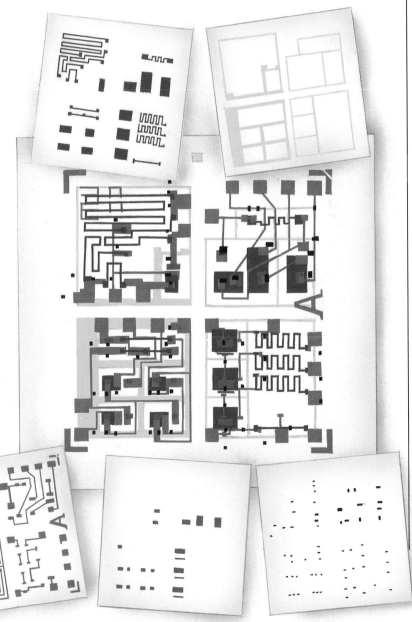

Above right: American geologists check the San Andreas fault in California. Portable computers quickly had many uses in field research, for storing and relaying data for later use.

The thin wafers of the microchip, with minute parts, are built up from layers of brilliantly designed miniature electronic components.

Playing games is a part of most people's lives. They are a way of learning or acquiring skills as much as helping to keep mental or physical faculties in good order. In 1928 games and how people played them began to interest a brilliant mathematician, John von Neumann. He published his theory of games in 1944. This work was crucial to the development of the computer and became the basis for much of the Western strategy through the Cold War. From early on games between people and electronic calculators or computers received publicity.

Testing computers

In 1946 a US Army private and a Japanese clerk competed to solve arithmetical problems. The American used an electronic calculator, the Japanese an abacus. The Japanese won every time. Doubts about reliance on computers continued though the 1960s. American computer workers hired a Dutchman Mr William Hein, who had a remarkable ability for mental calculation to check the 'image' they had of the correct result. In the 1960s the Americans set up war games on computer. This proved dangerous. During the 1970s America was twice put on full nuclear alert by faulty computer systems.

The use of computers for war games was a feature of the Cold War between the USA and USSR from 1947 to 1991, and was the basis for the movie *War Games* in the 1980s.

The computer game arrives

In 1972 the microchip crossed over from war games to popular games when Atari pioneered video games. The Japanese game *Pacman* appeared in 1976, it was soon followed by *Space Invaders*. Their success was enormous and arcades of computer games appeared across the world. In 1977 Japanese criminals were tempted to steal new American chips used for games. The USA realized the danger, since the same chips were used to control their nuclear warheads.

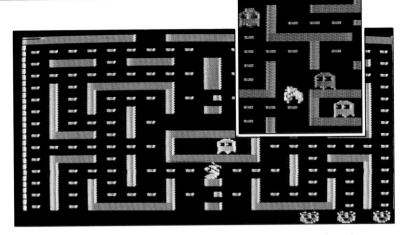

Early computer games, like *Pacman*, used simple graphics. Such games sold millions of copies.

Computer graphics and effects

The key to the development of computer games was the computer graphic. Computer-generated images were used in television from 1970, to explain complicated ideas. A range of computers and software were developed for schools. Graphics featured in the film *Westworld* in 1977. The film director George Lucas established 'Industrial Light and Magic' which evolved many of the computer film and video techniques for film and television used from 1980. In the late 1980s Sega and Nintendo introduced best-selling video games.

The success of computer games and graphics helped make computer technology widely acceptable. As a result, particularly in Japan, a whole range of products using visual displays (liquid crystal) and dedicated chips, which greatly increased efficiency and power were marketed at lower and lower cost. This revolution promoted Japan to the world's second largest economy in 1990. Computer-aided design became increasingly common, and was used to design shops, cars, kitchens and houses, directly influencing living conditions.

Home computing. The development of the personal computer made the machine accessible to a huge range of people in business and at home, using a variety of programmes including games.

A scene from *Star Wars*. George Lucas, the director of the *Star Wars* films, developed many of the modern computerized special effects used in television and movie productions.

MARKET CONTROL

The Wall Street crash of 1929 had serious consequences for much of the world. The world's leading trading system was close to collapse. Despite telecommunications there was a problem with the paper system and panic set in. The answer lay in improving electronic news systems. After the war, the growth in demand or need for pensions and insurance (especially for cars), as well as the introduction of universal social welfare systems and payment of earnings into bank accounts led to a huge rise in the circulation of money.

Computers in finance

The first commercial computers were used to keep records of repetitive information, such as payrolls for employees in large companies. Financial companies began to subscribe to news services provided by computer in the late 1950s. Then in 1958 a key decision was taken by US banks to encode all cheques in magnetic characters with the bank name and individual's account number. The first credit and charge cards soon appeared. These were followed by computer-controlled ATMs or automatic cash dispensers, giving access to cash 24 hours a day. All this movement of money provided a lot of information. The banks of knowledge built up were called databases. Governments began to use computers for a variety of checks – for tax, social welfare, surveillance, crime and to store and examine census data.

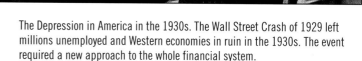

The Depression in America in the 1930s. The Wall Street Crash of 1929 left millions unemployed and Western economies in ruin in the 1930s. The event required a new approach to the whole financial system.

Computers in profile

As more personal data was stored it became possible to 'profile' a person, detailing almost everything about an individual through computer information. In the 1980s many governments saw this as a threat to liberty and passed laws to protect data access, as well as allowing some freedom to look at public computer records. As computers became central to financial systems, ciphers and codes largely replaced personal contact giving rise, from 1970 to ever-growing computer fraud. Computer-based finance had other worldwide effects.

Putting money to work

Banks joined their computers together in networks for central clearing of cheques and money. Stock markets were linked by computer, creating instant 'screen-based' trading, allowing dealers to be mobile. The old personal links were broken, which had important results. In 1987, the financial markets, which had switched to computer systems, suffered a huge shock when automatic 'sell' computer programmes in the USA caused the markets to fall rapidly. Share values plummeted causing the first ripple of the recession which was to hit the West in 1989.

Above right: In the 1980s the on-screen revolution in stock markets throughout the world greatly increased the use of computers in business, covering many aspects of daily life.

Signs and symbols, not that different from the hieroglyhics of Ancient Egypt, became the new international languages for computers in the 1980s.

The idea of robots has two origins. The first was an Italian invention of the 16th century – the mannequin used by artists to stand in for real people, which was made with similar joints to a living person. The second was a toy, powered by clockwork, to amuse children of the wealthy in 18th-century France, usually produced by master craftsmen to mimic natural movements. Until the 1920s these objects were seen as little more than amusements, even given the wide use of realistic dummies in shop windows.

R.U.R. The original robot was thought up by author Karel Capek in 1920 and was made later in the decade.

The invention of the robot

In 1920 Karel Capek's play *Rossum's Universal Robots* was staged. His vision of a future mechanical, or machine-person appealed to many people. A whole series of books, films and plays about robots appeared, including Fritz Lang's film *Metropolis*. Much of this was entertaining, but there was a serious side. Marie Curie's discovery of radium in 1903 and Professor Piccard's exploration of the upper atmosphere and the world of the deep ocean in the 1930s proved that mechanical extensions to man were necessary to make some discoveries possible or ensure safety. Progress was made with hard, plastic artificial limbs for soldiers maimed in World War I.

These became the model for a whole range of pincer-like instruments for use when handling dangerous materials. Robot technology was also applied from the 1920s in optics.

The rise of automation

A first usable telescope appeared in Holland in 1608. The success or failure of a telescope and related optical instruments depended on the accuracy of the curved lens used. The human eye and measuring instruments set limits on the size and quality of these lenses. The idea to use an automatic process to cut lenses came from robotics. During the 1930s, automatic control was introduced to a wide range of factory machinery. In the late 1930s the term was extended to cover domestic appliances and such objects as the automatic washing machine were heavily promoted.

By the 1980s developments in automation and optics led to large observatories, such as these in Australia and Russia, which probed the depths of space.

Robots as instruments of change

World War II widened the demand for optical instruments, from gun-sights to night cameras, from searchlights to range-finders on bombers. In 1944 an American devised a new rapid process of production called welding, which replaced laborious riveting. Since accurate fitting of parts was essential, automation became important and computer-controlled factory robots were introduced in many industries. Automatic robots are now used in many industrial processes, and have changed people's attitude to work and greatly affected employment throughout the industrialized world. Robots with the equivalents of eyes, hands and memory were used to explore the surface of Mars in 1976, to discover the wreck of the *Titanic* in 1981, to explore craters of volcanoes in 1992 and find two secret chambers in Egypt's Great Pyramid in 1993.

Fact or fiction – the android

In the 1950s robot toys were best-sellers. Walt Disney backed the development of animatronics for display at Disney World in 1965. Japanese scientists continued to work on more lifelike robots controlled by a series of chips. Out of this research came body parts including pacemakers and artificial limbs which respond to a person's own movements.

While tremendous advances have occurred, the making of a partial or whole android like the *Six Million Dollar Man*, *Robocop* or Dr Tryell's creations in *Bladerunner* remains distant.

Mars, as seen by a robot camera in 1976. Robots became crucial to the investigation of the planets and other areas which were too dangerous or distant for man to reach.

A robotic Dimetrodon dinosaur made in California. The use of robots in education and theme parks has enabled the past to be re-created in a way which helps our understanding of natural and human history.

Both language and art have used common signs as a basis for communication. Pictograms are images which refer to objects, such as stick men, and were used by all cultures for thousands of years. The connection of symbols – as words, then sentences – made understanding more complicated. By the 18th century, East and West had very different scripts. Science developed in two ways. One approach was based on proof or type of law. The other was indefinite, but possibly right – theories. Mathematics offered a way of presenting both using equations. This approach was common from about AD 200 worldwide.

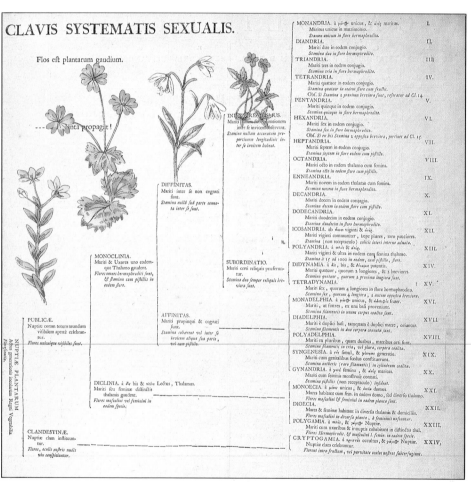

The need for new symbols

As scientists began to examine the natural world in the 1400s a system of common symbols and names was seen as useful. With the arrival of printing in the West these symbols became fixed. They joined to a new way of seeing – the art of perspective – representing, three-dimensional space. This system was largely evolved by the German artist Durer about 1480. As basic relationships between parts of the natural world were understood, 'families' or groups of structures were fixed by names, symbols and tables. The Swedish botanist Carolus Linnaeus drew up such a table for plants in 1737. In 1805 an Englishman, John Dalton, proposed a theory of atomic weights. To define his results Dalton set out the names of the 'elements' in Latin (the common language for Western scientists), symbols to represent them and numbers relating to the number of particles necessary to join elements.

The Table of Plants. Among the most important of the tables using signs was that of the Swedish botanist Linnaeus of 1737 which revealed the families of plants.

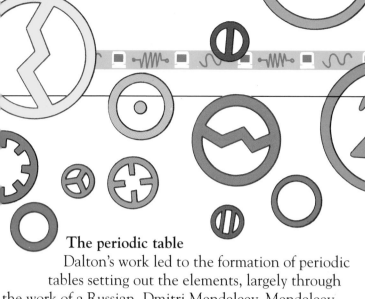

The periodic table

Dalton's work led to the formation of periodic tables setting out the elements, largely through the work of a Russian, Dmitri Mendeleev. Mendeleev saw that just as in a mathematical equation, there should be a balance in the groupings. If a balance did not exist then there was an element missing. It was symbols and numbers that made the idea possible to prove, first in theory and then in practice.

ELEMENTS

			W				W
☉	Hydrogen	1		✛	Strontian		46
◐	Azote	5		✳	Barytes		68
●	Carbon	5		①	Iron		50
◯	Oxygen	7		Ⓩ	Zinc		56
☮	Phosphorus	9		Ⓒ	Copper		56
⊕	Sulphur	13		Ⓛ	Lead		90
◉	Magnesia	20		Ⓢ	Silver		190
⊖	Lime	24		Ⓖ	Gold		190
◧	Soda	28		Ⓟ	Platina		190
▥	Potash	42		✺	Mercury		167

The Periodic Table of 1806. The table of the elements used Latin names and symbols. It featured only a small number of over 100 elements now known.

Discovering a world language

As new areas of scientific relationship or natural phenomena, such as electricity, were discovered a universal language was agreed, much of it based on arabic numerals, Latin names and common symbols. This made it possible for the interpreters of discovery – the engineers and technicians – to make useful products. Many of the signs and symbols in use today were fixed relatively recently – the main scientific symbols in 1881 and those for electrical diagrams and installation only in 1912. This system made approach to science easier and encouraged new forms of mathematics and signs. One of these, a new system of algebra called binary, was developed by an Irishman called Boulle in the 19th century. The binary number system uses only two digits, 1 and 0. In the digital computer all letters and numbers are translated to the code as strings of 1s and 0s. Another was the invention of a system of graphic tables by an Austrian, Otto Neurath – the isotype – in 1924. These two were to become crucial to the development of simple systems for the computer. Binary was adopted as the operating code, while the isotype was to form the basis of graphs and programs such as Windows.

The School of Athens by Raphael. A new way of presenting space in three dimensions, perspective was invented in the West in the 15th century.

The desire to understand the universe has been part of human history for centuries. This gave a focus for both religion and science, whose conflict helped to cause the weakening of influence of the Church in the West. The first manned exploration of the atmosphere was accomplished by balloons in the 18th century. By the end of the 19th century the elementary gases in air were known and the more distant worlds, those of galaxies, star clusters and planets were under ever closer observation by scientists.

Into space

Photography, analysis of reflected light from distant objects and theories of the likely physical behaviour of light and space all added to public interest in the subject by the late 1930s. A small number of scientists, among them Robert Goddard in the USA, Werner von Braun in Germany began experiments with liquid-fuel powered rockets (supercooled gas). Given the backing of the German Reich and a slave labour force, von Braun and his team launched the V1 and V2 flying bombs on arbitrary Western targets as an offensive weapon in 1944. They were terror weapons, pilotless and silent before impact. At the war's end the Allies seized all the data and personnel they could relating to the V1 and V2 rockets. The conquest of space became the goal for both the Russians and Americans. Two main types of craft were planned, the satellite and the rocket capable of carrying people.

The deadly V2 in flight. Fired from Germany and northern Europe in the last years of World War II, it was the most destructively successful of the early rockets.

Satellites and beyond

The satellite was proposed in 1949 by the science fiction writer and scientist Arthur C Clark. In the space race between the USA and USSR, huge resources were committed to the investigation of space and the development of atomic weapons systems based on rockets. The calculations for space travel to the moon and beyond, required high-capacity computers to work out the ideal flightpath and maintain contact with the craft. The invention of the microchip made the twinning of on-board computers with ground control possible. By the mid 1970s exploration of deep space by the US *Mariner* project and related observation brought understanding of the history and composition of the universe a little closer.

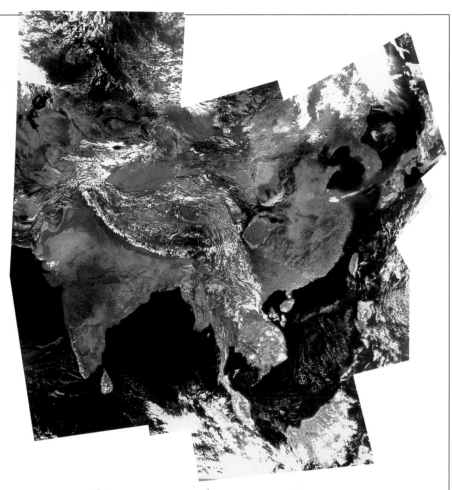

A satellite image of Asia, from Japan to the Caspian Sea, provides a whole range of information impossible to obtain without the use of rocket and computer sciences.

Building a global network

By 1980 satellites served to link nations, creating worldwide communications networks. Multinational projects such as Weathernet launched series of satellites to monitor the world weather systems; Computer graphics and databases modelled the likely conditions for weather bulletins. Computer-enhanced photographs, such as those of Mars in 1971, produced all manner of measurements from vegetation to water sources and from temperature to pollution. Databases and satellites are used to monitor animal populations, earthquakes and help locate natural resources. In 1988, using historical data, computers began to be used to design satellites and systems to process the continued flow of information.

Travel using satellite for navigation became very important for certain journeys, especially on the oceans, giving much more accurate positioning than was previously possible before the 1970s.

On constant watch

Many countries use satellites for continous surveillance, giving rise to extremely detailed 'spy in the sky' technology. It has been beneficial on the whole, making it virtually impossible for any country to make movements of its armed forces or threatening weapons without being observed.

Modern medical practice tries to minimize exterior infection and trauma. It had its beginnings in four wars in the 19th century where deaths from disease, shock and re-infection exceeded those of conflict. By 1914 the work of pioneers like Louis Pasteur of France and Robert Koch of Germany had solved the causes of major viral infections and the practice of immunization against a broad range of diseases was widely accepted. After the influenza epidemic of 1918, which is thought to have killed over 20 million people, vaccination against a variety of diseases became compulsory in many countries.

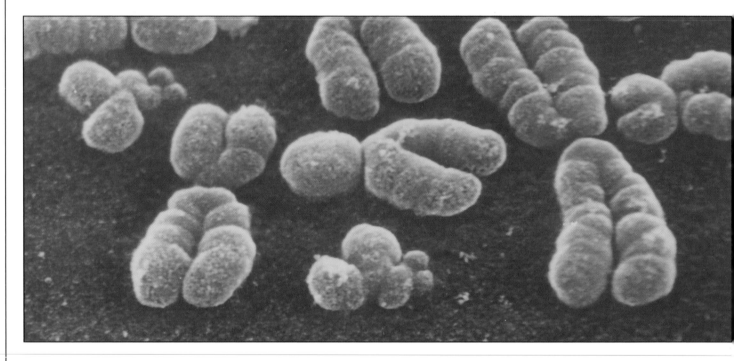

The chemistry of life

When Rutherford, Chadwick and Soddy identified electrons and neutrons, in England between 1902 and 1920, the possibility of micro-biology was opened up. By the 1930s the close examination of human and animal physiology began to unravel what was termed 'the chemistry of life'. This was one side of a dual exploration, the other was genetics. The chemical relationship between parts of a living organism and the structure of the cells opened the way to mass treatment of disease in humans. In 1932 two giant chemical and drug companies ICI in Britain and I G Farben in Germany were formed to exploit the new knowledge, dividing the world market between them. By 1945 these two strands of knowledge contributed to the Holocaust. Millions of people in camps such as Auschwitz, Dachau and Belsen had become mere numbers to be killed, or human guinea-pigs for unethical experiments.

An electron microscope photograph. It is coloured to help to reveal a new world beyond human sight. This image shows the key to genetic heredity – the chromosome.

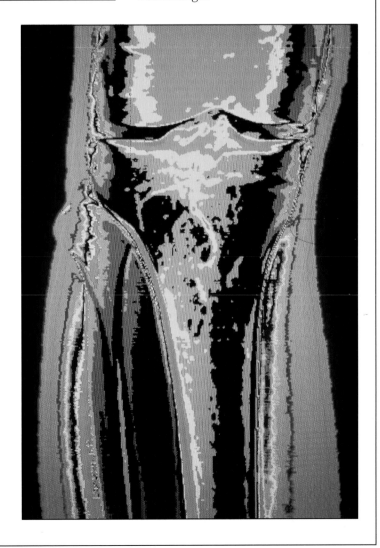
Oenothera albida,
eine jährlich auftretende Art.

DE VRIES, Mutation I. *Taf. 3.*

Examination of plants and their breeding patterns in the 19th century by Gregor Mendel led, with the aid of computers and atomic science, to a better understanding of the structure of many living things including DNA.

Body count

The basis of genetics was first explored by an Austrian monk, Gregor Mendel, in 1866. He defined such ideas as strains, character and hybrid. His numerical tables of probability and his lack of scientific training left him unrecognized for 40 years, when it was confirmed that inheritance is produced by the coupling of genes. It was not until 1953 that the answer to how inheritance is passed from one generation to another – DNA was discovered by Crick and Watson in Cambridge.

New medicine

Computers in health produced many breakthroughs, including the CAT scanner for brain and body scans, and the new science of genetic engineering. In the 1970s and 1980s these new methods led to the making of designer drugs, new surgical techniques and great strides in the understanding of the function of all creatures. These discoveries did, however, also raise serious questions about experimenting with life forms which remain unanswered.

Healthy combinations

This discovery coincided with the computer making it possible to examine graphics of molecular structure and genetic effects at speed, building models of likely relationships. This approach brought together science and the arts. From 1955 medical advances and practice became more international, involving world bodies, such as the World Health Organization, as much as private or public laboratories.

A CAT scan of a knee-joint showing the different temperatures of the various parts. These machines combining photography and computers reveal the inner workings of the body.

Since the typewriter could not produce columns, a different approach was needed. The rise of service businesses, those employing people who assist others, had increased demand for adding machines by 1888. That year two Americans A C Lundlum and William Burroughs found a solution, producing adding machines with full keys. In the 1870s small shops began to be replaced by new chains or department stores, among them such names as Sears, Harrods and Selfridges. These could reach markets of people more easily. With new laws requiring records of sales and the fact that managers no longer worked directly in the stores, but in an office, counters needed adding machines.

Counter revolution

The earliest machines in 1879 displayed price and change, but still needed staff to mentally calculate more than one sale. The introduction of handles and flat keys made it possible to calculate direct. These machines formed the basis of a new industry – gambling by one-armed bandits. In the USA large companies such as National Cash Register (NCR) came to dominate the market. Semi-automatic machines, giving receipts printed on paper appeared in the 1920s. These were adapted from gramophone technology and used electricity. Combination machines soon appeared, for counting coins, registering sales and doing accounts.

The invention of self service

The principle was applied to a whole range of self-service machines, from weighing scales to ticket machines. New businesses such as launderettes and drink-dispensing depended on them. The revolution broadened to the supermarket, where large ranges of goods appeared on a self-select basis. The checkout became a feature of their design. In the 1970s electronic cash registers were introduced, which later registered computer codes, or bar codes, on all retail products, allowing detailed information to be collected about sales.

The microchip also made it possible to develop similar products, including the pocket calculator. These used flat keys and liquid crystal displays. The calculator was immensely popular and led to the mini computer, among the first being Sir Clive Sinclair's ZX81, of 1981, which sold over a million. The two products were combined in the mid-1980s as the personal organizer. These products relied not only on design, but a light material, which was crucial to the development of modern electronics – plastic.

The Sinclair ZX81 of 1981. It was the first truly portable machine for a wide audience, it evolved from the calculator.

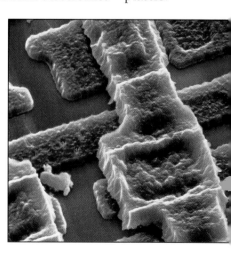

The arrival of the age of plastic

The first plastics were used for film – celluloid was invented in 1855 and made non-inflammable in 1894. Ten years later a Dutchman came up with a new material, Bakelite, only available in brown, which was both solid yet light. It was used on the first mass-market cameras and many other products. In 1926 the first coloured plastics appeared, shown at the Wembley exhibition, London. During the 1930s a new approach to making plastics, injection into moulds, made all types of shapes possible. The most common type of plastic was based on resins, derived from oil, which can be coloured. When miniaturization became possible, it was the ideal material for a great number of products.

The use of plastic in a whole range of everyday products led to improved design and an ideal material for miniaturization.

A silicon chip enlarged about 1300 times. The key to the new products of the retail revolution from the 1960s onwards was the silicon chip, with its ever larger memory.

Modern computers (*right*) can model buildings and play games. They can only get bigger and better.

When the US Army drove out the Nazis from Luxembourg in 1944 they discovered a new German tape recorder. Up until then American recording machines had been based on those of the Danish inventor Paulson, using metal wire to record sounds. The German tape was coated with ferric oxide (a form of rust) which ran through a magnetic head. At the same time, in California, a small company called Ampex was working on a visual recorder. It seemed unlikely that these machines might affect the way people lived in the future.

A German tape recorder of about 1944. It used plastic tape to record, the basis of the modern tape and video recorder.

Right: A Cray Supercomputer

The arrival of the supercomputer

In early computers punchcards were common. From the 1950s IBM experimented with tape-recorder technology, storing data on audio magnetic tape. Ordinary C15 (15-minute) blank cassette tapes became the original means of storage for the PC. The image of 'modern offices' with banks of computers headed by whirling tapes became familiar in the 1960s. The use of such mainframes required architects to redesign offices.

For some operations a single main-frame was insufficient. US political programmes required huge computer capacity to perform millions of calculations at speed giving rise to the supercomputer. Cray delivered the first of these to the Livermore Laboratory in 1962. Towards the end of the 1970s the immense capacity of supercomputers was sufficient to cover large-scale projects, including the preparation of animation film cells for the Disney cartoon-feature *Tron*.

Being very heavy, strong concrete floors supported by steel girders were needed to take the load. The huge trail of wiring required 'pockets' to run throughout the building. The heat generated needed to be taken away, making air conditioning and constant water flow necessary. Interconnection required an open plan. Lighting systems changed from bulbs to neon-strip tubes.

The most popular form of computer storage is the disc, capable of storing hundreds to thousands of pages of material.

Below right: Rock band Deep Purple in performance. Chip technology made stadium rock shows possible.

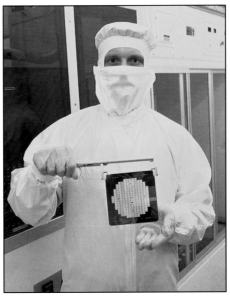

New ways of storage

The introduction of floppy discs and tape streamers to back up the hard-disc data increased the capacity of the personal computer. New ways of storing data were invented. One, was based on the music compact disc, CD-Rom; another, optical discs, were invented by Japanese and US companies. By 1988 new types of chip made cheap PCs closer in power to mainframe computers, and made a huge impact on the older, giant computer companies.

A world of change

Telephone, film, sound and video technology made equal rapid advances. Satellites had made distant audio-visual broadcasting possible in even remote islands by 1968. Worldwide television was pioneered by CNN through the 1980s, while video and photography adopted chip-based systems leading to the camcorder in 1982. Synthesized sound in electronic form had been pioneered by Dr Moog of the USA in the early 1960s, while invention of a new range of sounds came from electric guitar designers, such as Leo Fender. Digital and portable sound was launched in 1979 with the Sony Walkman and electronic DX7 sound. The communications industries made huge advances, using chips throughout their operations. In 1988 optical fibres and compression of data were linked, opening up new 'highways' for cable TV and picture phones. The next year Philips in Holland launched multimedia, a complete mix of sound, vision and text. A world network was beginning to be established.

The microchip has now been incorporated in millions of products and used as the basis of thousands of services. In the 1970s its use posed challenges for jobs. Competition between countries and companies for jobs increasingly required a free flow of imaginative ideas. One development from this was virtual reality. At the end of the 1980s the idea of imaginary worlds which were also 'real' became possible in computer memory. Great visionaries and leaders made the future happen in a similar way. The chip is so cheap it is almost worthless in itself but it is so widely used that society would collapse without it. Recent wars have has shown this is the case.

Dedicated chips

Basic supply systems to sustain or maintain daily life have introduced 'dedicated' chips. These chips do one job, which is pre-programmed. A TV remote control unit won't operate a video recorder and vice versa. Water and electricity supply rely on computers, controlling the supply and switching it to where it is needed. Fridges for food preservation, communications and thermostats for heating, air-conditioning systems for cooling similarly include chips. The exchange and use of money relies on electronic processing.

Maintenance of law and order increasingly relies on central computer data. Medical treatment and drug production is sustained by computers and related information technologies. Transport of people and goods depends on flight and supply systems. Knowledge of how computers or microchips work is not necessary to make use of the products. One of the most common uses is as a storage medium – preserving the past and preparing for the future.

The spread of computers

In 1982 experiments began in the USA with interactive systems, using cable links and television resulting in home shopping, remote auctions and property purchase. The combination of satellites and data is revealing considerable water and mineral resources, aiding pest control and land use surveys. DNA fingerprinting (which can indentify individuals at the scene of a crime by the DNA trace unique to each individual), synthetic drugs and genetic engineering, which now makes it possible to claim the rights to specially-bred animals, have become practical using chips. Many of these new applications have brought science and art closer together and undoubted benefits. Others raise questions.

The model and clone frog. Advances in computers and medical science makes cloning of species possible, copying the original many times over.

Problems emerge

The huge growth in video games has led to medical and social problems, genetic engineering has raised fears about 'Frankenstein' projects, synthetic drugs are seen as increasingly less acceptable, virtual reality has suggested that many may be tempted to live in a 'virtual' rather than a real world, new weapons have raised concern about reliance on advanced technology. Hacking and computer viruses can threaten lifestyle and livelihood.

Universal benefits

On balance, the microchip has been of enormous benefit, not least because conflict or secret activity becomes easier to monitor and reveal. In less than ten years, people have been able to make their own decisions in a way which makes dictatorship and intolerance less likely, but only where the technology remains with ordinary people. While it remains unlikely that an artificial intelligence will be possible in the near future, the applications and effects of the microchip will continue to increase.

A virtual reality session. The new vision allows direct involvement of the viewer in a world which exists only on computer, replacing the real world.

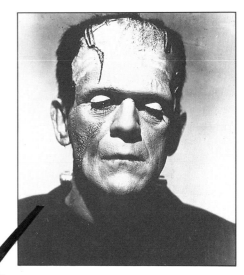

The image of Frankenstein – Boris Karloff. Rapid changes in genetic engineering made possible by computer has given rise to fears of real Frankenstein projects.

The Stealth Fighter Bomber. Advances in computer design and techniques in the 1980s resulted in new 'smart' weapons, among which was the American Stealth fighter, used in the Gulf War of 1991.

analogue The word used to describe any calculator which uses objects for arithmatic problems, such as the abacus, which uses beads on wires or strings.

android A robot or automated puppet which resembles a human being.

animatronics The name given to animated electronic figures, produced as either real objects or as pictures in a computer.

astrobale An instrument used by ancient astronomers, such as the Greeks, to measure the height of the stars and planets as an aid to navigation on either land or sea.

Babylonians People from the area of Mesopotamia (roughly modern Iraq and Syria) who settled in the region about 2000 BC.

census The number based listing of the population of an area of country, where the people live and the type of background of the people, such as the work they do.

ciphers Any of the Arabic numerals or images which represent numbers.

Cold War The name given to the historical period from about 1946 to about 1991 when there was a great difference in basic values between the East and the West, especially between the United States and the (then) Soviet Union.

computer enhanced This term is used for any image which has been improved or cleared up using computer.

digit Any numeral from 0 to 9; it is also applied to counting on either fingers or toes-digit by digit.

flightpath The standard plan for the direction of an aircraft flying from one place to another.

frequency The term given to a radio signal, which occurs regularly.

hybrid A plant or an animal which has been crossed or mated with another plant or animal which is not of the same type is known as a hybrid.

immunization The process of giving injections or tablets to prevent diseases which are transmitted between one person and another.

lathe A tool used from very early times to hold (and turn) wood or other material for carving or shaping at high speed.

Maya Indian peoples of northern South America whose civilisation was largely destroyed by 1600 AD. They were especially known for their temple complexes and knowledge of numbers and astronomy.

multinationals Companies which might have a central office but have branches in many different countries.

patent The listing, usually by law, of an idea or process which protects the invention or idea from use by others without permission.

payroll Any listing of payments due to people, such as wages or salaries. This can be for one or more than one company or group.

physiology The science of studying the way parts of living things work – for example, what they are made of.

product Usually the end result of a manufacturing process or farming, the word is also used to describe the adding of one number to another.

resins Thick treacle like sap or similar products from plants which occur naturally and can be hard or soft. In the 20th century made-up (synthetic) resins were produced.

strains The common link between different types of plants or animals which can be grouped together, often in "families".

telegraph The mechanical transmission of messages using a punch key at either end to send an electric signal down a series of wires.

telex The name given to an international telegraph service. It uses teleprinters to print out messages sent by telephone. During the 1980s it was often replaced by the fax machine.

tram Also known as a trolley, they are rail based public transport services, often using electricity from overhead cables.

trauma The result of a sudden shock. The shock could be mental or physical and could often be deadly.

virus Minute particles which attack all sorts of living creatures, being the source of many diseases. They can only survive in a host.

INDEX

A

abacuses 8, 10, 26
adding machines 38
airline industry 24
Apple 25
Arabic numerals 10
artificial limbs 31
Atari 27
ATMs 28
automation 30-1

B

Bakelite 39
banking 11, 28, 29
bases, numerical 8, 9
BASIC 25
binary system 23, 33
botanical table, Linnaean 32
business 18-19, 21, 25, 28-9, 42

C

calculators 11, 26
CAT scanners 37
CD-Rom 41
censuses 12, 13
chip, making of the 23, 25, 39
cloning of species 42
COBOL 20
codes 14-17, 19

D

databases 28, 35, 42
design, computer-aided 27
DNA 37
Domesday Book 12

E

education 27, 31
electron microscopes 22, 36
Enigma coding machine 17
espionage 15-17, 22, 35

F

Ferranti 20, 21
films 27, 30, 40, 41
financial companies 28-9
floppy discs 41
Fortran 20
fraud, computer 29

G

games, computer 27
genetics 36-7, 43
geometry 9
graphics, computer 24, 27

H

home computing 27

I

IBM 19, 20, 24, 39, 40
intelligence services 14-17
isotypes (Otto Neurath) 33

L

languages, computer 20, 25
logarithms 11

M

main-frame computers 19, 40
maps 13
mathematics, early 8-11, 32
medical sciences 13, 36-7, 42
microbiology 36-7
miniaturization 22, 39
modems 25
Morse Code 15
multimedia 41

N

navigation 35

O

oil refining 21
optical discs 41

P

pacemakers 31
Periodic Table 33
perspective, art of 32, 33
photography 22, 34, 41
plastics 38-9
pocket calculators 38
portable computers 25
'profiles' 29
punchcards 11, 13, 40

R

radio 15-17
railways 18
robots 30-1
rocket technology 34

S

satellites 35, 41, 42
scanners 37
self-service machines 38
shorthand 14
Sinclair ZX81 38
slide rules 11
social science 13
sound technology 41
space exploration 34-5
stock markets 29
storage, data 20, 41, 42
stores/supermarkets 38
supercomputers 40
synthesized sound 41

T

tabulators 13
tape recorders 40
telephones 15, 16, 21, 25
telescopes 8, 30
television 27, 41
Texas Instruments 22
transistors 21, 22
transport/travel 11, 42
typewriters 18-19, 38

V

video technology 41